# 44 Ways
## to Grow Your
## Business or Brand

Mavis Amankwah

44 WAYS TO GROW YOUR BUSINESS OR BRAND
– 1st Edition

ISBN: 978-0-9566665-2-9

Editing, Concept & Design Team
Darey Wealth. O
Nigel Graber
Ned Hoste
Michelle Adabra
Trisha Daniell

This book can be ordered from the Author or Publisher.
Author: www.mavisamankwah.com
www.richvisions.co.uk

Strides Publishing – A Part of Strides Media
www.stridesmedia.com

# 44 Ways to Grow Your Business or Brand

## Mavis Amankwah

# Contents

# Foreword

The textbooks tell you to make your business plans, to put aside cash in case it all goes belly up, and to be prepared for obstacles and high hurdles. I'd read those books and I had it all mapped out. Deep down, though, I didn't know if my business would survive five months, let alone five years. Then came the credit crunch and, suddenly, five weeks seemed more realistic.

Yes, the first five years are all about survival. It's been a rollercoaster ride, but I'm still here – sane, smiling, ready for action and as passionate and determined as ever to make my businesses succeed.

Whatever else I could say about those first few years, the one thing that's kept my business growing has been constant marketing and PR. The other thing I've proved myself good at is admitting I can't do everything. That means getting in professionals to implement and re-implement ideas.

So, if any aspiring business owner out there is looking for a five-year plan, this is it. This book is designed to help you survive for five years and beyond by ensuring your organisation is sound, effective, efficient and capable of weathering the storms of modern commerce.

Apart from those 44 marketing and promotional techniques you can use to sustain and grow your business, I'll be sharing the mistakes I've made – so that you can avoid them. But what else does this book offer?

Well, it focuses on growth. Yes, a clutch of top awards, being named as one of the most influential people in PR for three consecutive years, and building up a team of fifteen says I know how to run a business. Yet, when I started out in 2002, I made the mistake of putting growth on the backburner. My goals were Big Hairy Audacious ones (BHAG), but I wasn't backing them with action.

If only I'd had a book like this in my top drawer. It wouldn't have prevented those high hurdles from popping up, but it would have helped me leap over them without falling flat on my face.

Ultimately, I intend to show how, with the right people and the right advice, you can have a successful and sustainable business that will deliver a profitable concern you can sell, or a legacy you can leave behind.

If you're a young entrepreneur, a new and established small business or a sole trader, there'll be advice in this book for you. If you're involved in a community or faith organisation, you can draw strength from my experiences. If you want to increase your profile or expand your marketing and publicity efforts but don't have the know-how, please step this way.

# Acknowledgements

*"I can accept failure – everyone fails at something.*
*But I can't accept not trying."*
**Michael Jordan, basketball legend and businessman**

## My family
I would like to take this opportunity to thank God Almighty for keeping his eye on The Sparrow (that's me). No matter what obstacles I have faced, you have always shown up, even at the last hour when things looked bleak.

I would also like to thank my wonderful husband, Richmond Agyekum, who has been there through thick and thin, and my kids, Tevin and Tyarna, who have grown up to be obedient and helpful. Thanks to my mum, Dora Karikari, my stepfather, Tony Karikari, and my two brothers, Desmond and Nicholas, for just being there. To all my endless extended family and friends, thanks for all your love and consistent support through the years.

## Business
I would like to thank Reggae Reggae Sauce Business Entrepreneur Levi Roots for lending a listening ear, Tunde Alabi,ex-Business Link , Femi Okutubo, Trumpet Newspaper, Jennifer Kumi, Ruth Kagua and Delali Foli at Rich Visions, who are now part of the furniture, Nigel Graber for the quick turnaround of the text, Michelle Adabra for the great ideas on the book cover, Darey Wealth, the publisher, for being so patient, my good friend/business pal, Trisha Daniell (Digital Typist UK), and all the wonderful ladies at Rich Visions past

and present.

A big thank you to everyone, including all those who have done, and continue to do, business with me.

### Who this book is for

This book is for new or established businesses, managers of charities and not-for-profit organisations, up and coming entrepreneurs, social enterprises, mumpreneurs, business students, and sole traders in <u>any sector</u> who need to ramp up their marketing, PR and publicity efforts to increase their bottom line or revenue.

# Prologue: Black ties and beginnings

*"High achievement always takes place in the framework of high expectation."*
**Charles Kettering**

"And the winner is…"

Those are words I never thought I'd hear in real life. Awards ceremonies were once as foreign to me as space travel. But here I was in one of London's Hiltons, surrounded by local notaries in black ties and cocktail dresses, waiting to hear if I'd won one of the most prestigious business awards in town.

When Pam Joseph announced my name, I nearly screamed. Then, when I spoke on stage, it was all about young people – I dedicated the award to the youngsters I'm lucky enough to work with and thanked the organisers for their generous support of local youth.

Although I'm not one to blow my own trumpet, when I reflected on the award later, it did seem like just reward for all that I'd been through. While this was the second of three big awards, and I've been named as one of the most influential people in Public Relations for three consecutive years, life wasn't always like that.

While I initially trained in PR, until 2004 I was working as an IT Manager. But I was struggling to keep up with the technology and, frankly, had no passion for my job. I'd wanted to work for myself for as long as I can remember. I'd moonlighted on some PR work in the community and it seemed like a natural move. Even my old boss backed me. So I researched the market, launched a pilot and my integrated communications agency, Rich Visions, took off back in 2002.

I guess you could say I'm driven by adversity. I was born into a tough East London suburb in 1974 and raised by my mum and, later, my stepdad, when my dad left at an early age. I put up with racial abuse and name-calling at school. An Irish teacher told me that I'd 'never amount to anything'. I had those words ringing in my ears that night in the Hilton.

It was my mother who made me stronger. She always worked hard to support our family, and I inherited her values. My mum also had great dignity – in an era of huge prejudice. She still recalls signs in the windows of rented accommodation saying, 'No blacks, Irish or dogs'.

My resolve was also hardened by a couple of childhood incidents that are outside the scope of this book. Perhaps I'll document them elsewhere. Suffice it to say, they were pretty horrific. But, again, they made me stronger.

But this book isn't about me. It's about giving practical advice on how you can walk the walk I walked, dodge the bullets I dodged, and use marketing and PR to systematically grow your business. I hope you find it useful.

# One: Ideas and infrastructure

*"Disneyland is a work of love. We didn't go into Disneyland just
with the idea of making money."*
**Walt Disney**

If you're just starting out, this chapter's for you. We all have to
start somewhere and planning is obviously a key element. Here's
my seven-point checklist for any aspiring business owner.

### 1 Have a great business idea

First things first. It might seem obvious, but you do need a
workable business idea. When you're first starting out in your
business, you need to know what you want to do and why
you want to do it. The idea you have will usually stem from a
personal passion.

Some people start a business because they just want to make
money, and that's fine. However, I strongly believe that passion
should be the main priority, followed by money. That's because
you can make money through a number of different channels
and you don't necessarily have to run a business to make money.

Read about high-profile entrepreneurs – such as Peter Jones
or Deborah Meaden from TV's Dragons' Den – and you'll see
that they all started with an idea that they were passionate
about. Peter Jones's first love was tennis – and his first business
venture was a tennis academy, when he was just 16.

You might still be working for someone else when you have
your business idea. That's fine. Start putting all your plans
and ideas together. Consider the type of customers or clients
you're looking for. One mistake I made was to try and focus on
one particular target audience. It took me about three years to

11

realise that I needed to look in to new markets and diversify.

This factor – researching new markets and looking at new target audiences – has really helped my business to grow today. To survive a recession, you must diversify – before, during and after. The other vital factor when starting or expanding your business is research – lots of it. Just writing a business plan won't sustain you for the long-haul without facts or intelligence.

Always make your ideas and plans BHAG (Big Hairy Audacious Goals). Imagine an idea that is beyond your skills, knowledge and capability. Your BHAG idea and plan should be out of this world. Don't be afraid to think BIG, as anything is possible. Remember, if you shoot for the stars, you might at least hit the moon.

But please make sure your business idea is viable and feasible ensuring you write up your strategy and ideas into a business plan. Speak to somebody, a professional who's been in business for a long time. Tell them your idea or what you are thinking of inventing, creating or developing, and then look at people who are offering similar products and services. Look at what they're already doing and pick it up or learn new techniques. Consider their business's experiences and structures. Find out everything you can about what they did or are doing to make their business prosper.

For me, I realised there was a niche in the market where I could get mainstream organisations to look at tapping into diverse audiences. Today, my company, Rich Visions, has grown from a one-woman band to an award-winning enterprise.

## 2 Have a Unique Selling Point

It would be tough to find a marketplace that wasn't crowded these days. So the trick is to stand out from your competitors.

Or at least appear to do so. I love to use this example to explain a USP simply.

Imagine you're in a room where everyone is trying to sell you oranges. But you can afford to buy just one orange. So now you have to decide whose orange to buy, based on a number of factors. One guy's oranges are from Southern California, someone else's are grown locally, and one lady says hers are juicier.

But the one that you'll buy will be the one that attracts you the most and fits your own personal preference. Without some kind of point of difference, you won't be able to choose an orange.

So look at what's unique. Without a USP, people have no reason to buy from you.

My company's USP is the fact that we can help our clients reach diverse markets. But life is never that simple – because my competitors would say the same thing. However, our uniqueness comes from being able to target by religion, by ethnicity or by disability. If we get into ethnicity, we can even go into countries and tribes and generations. A lot of our competitors don't do that. That's BHAG thinking.

---

**Ask yourself**

If you have an idea, write it down and start working on the idea. Ask yourself the following questions:
- What is my idea?
- Why do I want to do it?
- What do I want to achieve?
- Where do I want my business idea to be in three years' time, five years' time and 15 years' time?
- Do I have the time?
- Do I have the energy?
- Am I ready for the challenge?

## Look at big companies

So, what's *your* USP? One way of finding out is to take a look at some huge organisations or brands that you like and see how quickly you can identify their USP. What makes you buy from them or keeps you going back to use them? International brands tend to use their USP in their advertising, so the message to customers and potential customers never stops. It's all about differentiation from the rest.

A fine example is the breakdown recovery service, the AA (Automobile Association). For some time, the AA used the slogan, 'To our members, we're the fourth emergency service' (after the police, fire brigade and ambulance).

With this choice of strapline, the AA is showing clearly how valuable and trusted they are to their members. Their USP states that they regard vehicle breakdowns as emergencies, and react accordingly. Their slogan states quite clearly why potential members should choose them over other breakdown recovery services.

### 3 Get yourself a mentor

Mentors are really important in business. They have the experience and skills, they've been there before and they've worn the t-shirt. They can give you the advice you need to sustain your business.

Business isn't just about money – money to invest here or pay for that. Some things can't be bought, which is where your mentor comes in. For me, having a mentor has been one of the most important elements in the success of my businesses. My mentor can see loopholes and gaps, provide advice, encourage me, motivate me, and let me see the bigger picture.

## 4 Understand the legal structure of your business

Very few people start their business with much of a thought about its legal structure. Do you want to be a social enterprise? Does your business need to be trademarked? Do you want to be a sole trader? Do you want to set up as a limited company or as a community interest company?

The choice is yours, but you need to think about the structure that works for you. If you're unsure, there's lots of information out there on the Internet, at your local business chamber or in the library.

**Here's a little more information.**

**Sole trader**
Sole trading means keeping things simple. You won't need to pay registration fees, and your accounting should be pretty easy. You also keep all those lovely profits. On the downside, you're responsible for your business's debts.

**Partnership**
Partnerships come in three flavours: 'ordinary' partnerships, limited partnerships and limited-liability partnerships. With all of them, two or more partners share the risks, responsibilities, profits and gains. Each partner pays their own tax and share of the profits.

**Starting a private company**
A private limited company and private unlimited company are the two types of private company. Limits according to shares or a guarantee can be set for a private limited company. Private companies have to be registered (incorporated) at Companies House.

**Starting a public limited company**

Public Limited Companies (PLCs) keep the finances of the company separate from the members' personal finances. PLCs must have two shareholders at least and have issued a minimum of £50,000 of shares. They must have two directors and a secretary and be registered (incorporated) at Companies House.

**Buying a franchise**

If all that sounds like just too much of a risk, how about starting a franchise? That way, you can take advantage of an established, successful business. You'll buy a licence to use the name, products and services of the business in a confined geographical area.

## 5 Have a sound grasp of business finances

Business is about money, and one of the most important elements is understanding the financial side of your business. That means keeping tabs on your cashflow, your profit and loss, and your balance sheet. Understand your finances and where you are with them. It's so easy to shrug and say, "Yes, my accountant has my books," or "I have an accountant or bookkeeper."

But, your business is *your* responsibility. If you're the business owner, you need to have those accounts with you at all times. You need to know whether you're making a profit or a loss and know where you can increase sales and revenue. Your finances should be robust.

## 6 Get a little black book and fill it

Business these days is all about contacts, contacts and contacts.

Preferably good ones. Great contacts range from your bank manager to people who can help you build an effective website, to networking contacts who can drive more business your way.

Over the past seven years, I've managed to build up a real network of reliable contacts so that I can grow my business. It's vital that you do the same so you can contact the right people at the right time.

## 7 Get ready to diversify in hard times

In tough times, it's diversify or die. Your industry might have been struck by a recession, but that doesn't mean you have to give up. The key is to diversify.

Let's imagine you're a beauty therapist offering just one service to your clients. Why not look at what other services or products you can offer? They don't have to be anything needing an investment of much money or time; they can simply be an add-on. If you offer back massages, why not offer hand massages or head massages, too? If you're a photographer, consider providing video services as well.

Or perhaps, if your industry is quiet at the moment, you need to look at a different market, rather than closing your business down because you think there's no market for your product or services right now. Instead, think: who else could be interested in your offerings in a different market? How do you get into that market?

In today's markets, diversifying is one way of spreading the risk, adding another income stream or simple increasing your sales. You have three options – you'll need to find:

☐ Products or services for existing customers.
☐ Customers for existing products/services.

☐ Services or products for new markets.

To an extent, diversification can protect you from threats you can't control (social and economic), but it can also have a negative effect on your business. You need to plan strategically and not just rush into things without weighing the risks against the benefits.

So, get out of your comfort zone and look at different markets and sectors. There'll be a need for your product or service somewhere in the market. There are always opportunities for new markets. It's just a case of researching and identifying where new opportunities lie.

## 8 Don't waste space on your business cards

A business card is one of the first essential items your business needs. Of course, you'll need all your contact details on there, including landline number, mobile number, address, website URL, Twitter accounts, Facebook accounts – don't skimp on ways you can be contacted.

When you give your email address, make sure it's the one linked to your website – it'll make you look much more professional than a free Hotmail or Yahoo address.

That professionalism and trustworthiness also extends to phone numbers, which is why you should always ensure your landline number appears on your card. A business card with just a mobile number always looks a little fly-by-night and will trigger doubt in your contact's mind. In any case, these days, you can get landline numbers that can be diverted straight to your mobile.

As regards addresses, if you work from home and don't want to give your personal address on your business card, that's fine.

However, ensure that you provide your mobile and a landline. If you do list your personal address, be very careful, or buy yourself a mailing address. Note that PO Box numbers don't look professional enough any more and always raise suspicions among your contacts.

These days, there are so many mailing addresses you can buy for a reasonable price that it just makes sense to do so. You can even have West End or city addresses like Mayfair or Regent Street, which give your business lots of lovely credibility. So what's stopping you?

One more important element of your business card that's often overlooked is the back: leave it blank and you miss a great opportunity to say something about your business. How about a list of products or services? A special offer? A strapline or maybe a mission statement? Remember: business is about maximising your opportunities.

## 9 Always conduct competitor analysis

Conducting competitor analysis can help you assess the strengths and weaknesses of your existing and potential competitors. This can help you identify opportunities and threats in your industry sector.

A detailed competitor analysis will play several important roles in your strategic planning. You'll better understand your competitive advantages and disadvantages in relation to your competitors. You'll also get a grasp of your competitors' past, present and (most importantly) future strategies.

Your analysis should give you an informed basis on which to develop strategies to achieve competitive advantage in the future. You'll also be able to forecast the returns that can be made from your future strategies and investments.

As a starting point, try answering the following questions:

- [ ] Who are your competitors?
- [ ] What threats do they pose?
- [ ] What is your competitors' profile?
- [ ] What are your competitors' objectives?
- [ ] What strategies are your competitors using and how successful are they?
- [ ] What are your competitors' strengths and weaknesses?
- [ ] How much are they charging for their products or services?
- [ ] How are your competitors likely to respond to changes in the way you do business?

Don't base your analysis on industry gossip or assumptions. This kind of competitor analysis gives you concrete facts to base your marketing strategy on. Over the years, I've seen lots of companies (big and small) not doing enough of this analysis. With patchy or incorrect information, you might have some major 'blind spots' on your competitors, which can put you at a distinct disadvantage.

## 10 Get used to networking

Networking is the art of getting to know people. It's been constant networking that has helped me win contracts and new business. I've widened my business circles and created new opportunities, and you can do the same.

There are no right or wrong ways to go about networking, but you should ensure that your networking always has an objective or motive. It might be lovely to chat over a glass of wine in a room full of pleasant people, but if they're never going to be in business, they'll never refer your products or services.

But what's better? Face-to-face or online networking? Only you can decide which is better for you. If you're painfully shy, perhaps take your first networking steps online by registering on websites like LinkedIn, Ecademy, Facebook or Twitter.

Set up your (or your company's) profile, include all your relevant information and get connecting. Start with people/ businesses you already know and have relationships with. Then cast your net a little wider by connecting with the contacts of your contacts. You can also request 'virtual' introductions to people you'd like to connect with and invite new people to join you and sign up to your group or fan page.

Before you know it, you'll be networking like a professional from the comfort of your home or office. Then, once you've gained some confidence, you can move from meeting in a virtual environment to meeting people face to face. Remember: practice makes perfect.

One vital thing to remember is that networking isn't solely a way of getting new business. See it as a method of expanding on your business experience, creating relationships that could be beneficial to your business and of raising your profile. Last and not least – it's a way of giving something to others. Remember: if nobody gave, nobody would receive.

## 11 Make sure you're charging the right price or fee

A lot of research shows that many business owners underprice their products or services. In theory, you might think the company operating at the lowest price will do the best business. But, in truth, the highest-priced business might be selling the highest number of units or doing the most business.

As a general rule, you should charge as much as possible for your product or services. But there are many factors to consider before deciding on your price, for example:

- [ ] The type of customer you're targeting.
- [ ] Competition in your industry or marketplace.
- [ ] Whether you're selling for cash or credit.
- [ ] Whether you accept returns, or give guarantees.

Of course, you can offer the lowest prices on the planet. But that will probably mean giving up the attractive services that your competitors offer. These could be personal attention, free delivery, replacement of faulty goods, refunds, and/or easier credit terms. If you don't offer such services, you might lose the customers or clients who want them and are happy to pay for them.

Being cheaper is not always the best option. You may also be perceived as having a poorer-quality product or service, which can deter some buyers. Consider your target audience, your level of skill, your experience or the quality of your product and price accordingly.

Adopt what's known as a 'pull strategy', in which you carefully explain what your products and services can do for your clients, before you tell them what they'll cost.

Later in this book (under SWOT Analysis), you can read about my company's weaknesses a few years ago. When we carried out our SWOT analysis, we discovered one of our weaknesses was that we were undercharging for a long time to win business.

This resulted in not being able to make a profit for a very long time. Some potential clients also decided that, because we were too cheap, our service must not be the bee's knees, so decided to try out our competition instead.

## 12 Have a slick elevator pitch

Being in business means keeping your eyes open for every opportunity. That means being able to answer key questions very quickly. What does your company do? Who do you sell to? How many services do you offer?

This is where the elevator pitch comes in. Imagine you're in a lift with Bill Gates. You're both going to the top floor. You have until then to explain to him all about your business. Let's say roughly 30 seconds to one minute.

That might sound easy. But try it in front of a mirror. It's probably harder than you think. Having a perfect (and rehearsed) elevator pitch means you'll always be <u>professionally</u> prepared. I underline the word professionally as too many people are quick to tell you what they do, but go into a huge spiel about their personal background, qualifications and status.

So, the message is: stick to what's relevant. Get to the point by telling Mr Gates your name, your company and what you do before you get to that penthouse suite. Then ask him what he does.

# Two: Marketing and messaging

*"Marketing is too important to be left to the marketing department."*
**David Packard**

## 13 Understand what marketing's all about

**Ask yourself**

When working on your marketing to grow your business, ask:

☐ What do you need to do to effectively market your business or brand?
☐ What cost-effective marketing methods can you use?
☐ Can you draft a simple, step-by-step marketing plan that anyone in your business can implement if you're away?
☐ Who are you going to be marketing to and how?
☐ How do you attract new customers and keep existing ones?

How do you promote and publicise your business or brand through marketing? At one of my workshops, I asked delegates if they could tell me what 'marketing' was. Replies included:

"It's about promoting your product."
"It's using different tools to reach your target audience."
"It's about creating awareness and more revenue."

Let's ask the Chartered Institute of Marketing. The CIM says: 'Marketing is crucial for business success. If you don't pay attention to what you sell, what prices you charge, what you're promoting and where you're going to sell them, your company is going to be unable to survive.'

Every day, it seems that even seasoned marketers are struggling to look at the issues around marketing and to define what marketing's all about. It's not really enough to place an ad in the paper, sit back and say 'Right, I've done my marketing. Why am I not getting any calls?'

Take a lesson from the big hitters – the big boys and big firms market themselves all the time. They're constantly looking at different ways to market themselves effectively.

At my company, we're always changing our marketing strategies. We look at what's worked and what hasn't worked, as well as how we're going to improve, how we're going to develop and how we're going to save money. We also regularly monitor and evaluate how much we're spending.

Saving money is an important part of the process. It's about spending more in areas that bring a greater return and less in those that don't. It's about paying attention to what we sell, our prices, and then looking how and where we'll market and promote our products, services, events and brand.

---

**Ask yourself**

Are you doing any type of marketing? Just take two minutes to write on paper the different types of marketing activities you're doing or thinking of doing over the next three, six, twelve months or two years.

---

## 14 Always market and promote yourself effectively

At one of my recent marketing workshops, I asked delegates why so many businesses are failing to market and promote themselves effectively. Here are some of the responses:

"They don't have a marketing plan or PR plan."
"They see marketing as a low priority."
"They think they have to get the business off the ground first before thinking about marketing."
"Marketing and PR are inconsistent."
"They don't have the know-how."
"They believe they have no competitors and there's no need to worry as 'people will come to me'."
"They can't define their Unique Selling Point (USP)."
"They're not using the right marketing mix."
"They don't have a budget for marketing."
"They're targeting the wrong people."

So, in summary – always have a marketing or PR plan, keep your efforts consistent, never go into business without a USP, and put aside a healthy budget for promoting yourself.

## 15 Always set yourself a marketing budget

No matter what type or size of business you run, I always say to organisations that you need to invest in some type of marketing and promotion. Whether it's a budget of 2% or 5% of your sales revenue, it's critical that you invest and consistently market your business. Evaluate and re-evaluate what's working and what's not working. Constantly throw money at your marketing. And always think: BHAG.

## 16 Understand the importance of your marketing plan

Your marketing plan is just as important as your business plan. What does the marketing plan do? Well, in summary, it:

- ☐ Tells you where you are now and where you'd like to be.
- ☐ Tells you how you're going to get where you want to be.
- ☐ Offers an insight into your clients, your competitors and your suppliers.
- ☐ Creates an action plan with a realistic timeline.
- ☐ Helps you budget.
- ☐ Helps you with strategies and tactics.
- ☐ Helps you understand the tools you need to implement the strategy or tactic.

It's a popular idea that 50% of marketing and advertising is wasted. The trouble is, you don't know which 50%. With a marketing plan, you can monitor what you're doing all the time and see what's working and what's not. The plan will help you co-ordinate your marketing efforts, reach your marketing goals and aspirations, and keep you on course.

The good news is that there are loads of templates out there to get you started on your marketing plan. Here's one of my own.

## RV MARKETING PLAN SAMPLE

| ACTIVITY | HOW | WHY | WHEN | DURATION | DESCRIPTION | RESOURCES | BUDGET | QUARTER |
|---|---|---|---|---|---|---|---|---|
| Social Media | | | | | | | | |
| Social Media Marketing | | | | | | | | |
| Article and Blog Distribution | | | | | | | | |
| Email Marketing Management | | | | | | | | |
| Facebook | | | | | | | | |
| Twitter | | | | | | | | |
| Website | | | | | | | | |
| Blog | | | | | | | | |
| RSS | | | | | | | | |
| Existing Database | | | | | | | | |
| Virals | | | | | | | | |
| PR | | | | | | | | |
| Video Clips | | | | | | | | |
| Marketing Material | | | | | | | | |
| E-Flyer | | | | | | | | |
| Calendar | | | | | | | | |
| Pop-up stands | | | | | | | | |
| Credentials | | | | | | | | |
| Brochures | | | | | | | | |
| Business Cards | | | | | | | | |
| Memory Stick | | | | | | | | |
| Promote To | | | | | | | | |
| E&D | | | | | | | | |
| Sector Skills | | | | | | | | |
| NHS | | | | | | | | |
| PCT | | | | | | | | |
| Training/ Events | | | | | | | | |
| Seminars | | | | | | | | |
| Workshops | | | | | | | | |
| Masterclasses | | | | | | | | |
| In House Training | | | | | | | | |
| Networking Events | | | | | | | | |
| Other | | | | | | | | |
| Speaker opps | | | | | | | | |
| Award Nominations | | | | | | | | |
| Newsletter & Marketing | | | | | | | | |
| Press Conference | | | | | | | | |
| Market Research | | | | | | | | |
| Referrals | | | | | | | | |
| Website | | | | | | | | |
| Visit top US | | | | | | | | |
| PR Angles | | | | | | | | |
| Free diversity calendar | | | | | | | | |
| Equality Bills | | | | | | | | |
| Flex Assessment | | | | | | | | |
| Census 2011 | | | | | | | | |
| Use mainstream press | | | | | | | | |
| Olympic2012 | | | | | | | | |
| E-Markets | | | | | | | | |
| Constant Contact | | | | | | | | |
| Newsletter | | | | | | | | |
| Email Capture | | | | | | | | |
| Website | | | | | | | | |
| Update contact | | | | | | | | |
| CMS | | | | | | | | |
| Database | | | | | | | | |
| transfer emails to cc | | | | | | | | |
| Roadshows | | | | | | | | |
| Feb-May: London | | | | | | | | |
| Sep-Nov: Bham, Leeds, Manchester, Bristol | | | | | | | | |

Your plan just needs to be simple and to the point. As long as you understand it and can explain it to somebody else, it doesn't matter what format it's in or how fancy the presentation is.

## 17 Put time into good market research

Before you even think about compiling your marketing plan, you need to conduct market research. It's all about collecting and analysing data about a particular target market.

You conduct market research to establish who your customers are, where they are and what they do. You also need to know what you need to do to reach and market yourself to them. Market research will also determine who your competitors are and what they're doing at the moment. It might also prompt questions like: can I offer my existing customers more? Are my current customers happy?

The key in today's competitive markets is understanding your audience. With certain sectors shrinking, it's key to know exactly how to get directly into a given market. How can you reach certain people?

Yes, the credit crunch might be alive and kicking in certain sectors of society, and everyone's saying they don't have two pennies to rub together. But the world's still turning and people are still spending money, even if some are working on a shoestring budget. We're all still putting petrol in our car, still buying clothes, still eating and still doing business.

We're all still doing what we have to do. It's just that we're being more strategic and clever and thinking things through before we dip our hands in our pockets, which is a good thing. For the marketer, it's a case of being a little bit smarter, understanding potential and actual clients, and then increasing our efforts in those particular markets. This is why research is really, really important.

You can spend £50,000 or £50 on your market research. It all depends on what and how much information/data you require. But here's an idea: there are lots of university students who conduct research projects for their assignments and dissertations. How about contacting a university to see if they have students who can help you do some research? As I say, it all depends on what you need and how much you have to spend.

### Desk or field research?
Which will you do?

- Interviewing people at shopping centres or on the street (field research)
- Collecting data by conducting research over the Internet (desk research).

### Types of research you require
Perhaps you want to conduct research over the telephone on the last seminar or workshop you did. Were the attendees happy? Is

there any way you could improve the event (there's always room for improvement in business)? Maybe you could also carry out the same activity face-to-face in a focus group or online.

I always find the easiest way to get basic data or information is the focus group, as they aren't very expensive. It's simply a case of getting the people you think are interested in what you have to offer into a room (although it's best not to use friends or your Aunty Beth), providing an incentive (like money or a clothes voucher) to attend, and then collecting the relevant feedback or information.

Research is vital to staying in business and many organisations are missing a trick by not doing any from the outset.

Research will also be beneficial if you're already in business but wanting to launch a new venture or expand your business. Research can help you find out what other services or products you can bring to the marketplace.

I try to do research into my competitors on a regular basis, just to see what they're doing and what I can do differently to become a market leader in my industry.

I always recommend conducting research in small doses. The questions you should ask yourself are: What do I want to find out at the moment? Why do I want to find that out? Is it because I need to get more sales? Is it because I need to get more people?

Ask yourself all of these questions, and then ask: What do I already know? What don't I know? What do I need to find out?

### Research in action

A few years ago, I had to go back to the drawing board for my business on our strapline. My team and I had realised that our logo and strapline didn't represent what we do. Our strapline stated that we did ethnic marketing and PR. However, we also cater for general marketing and PR.

We did some research – simply by asking our existing and previous clients what they thought about the colours, strapline, font style and so on. The feedback we received led to a complete overhaul of the logo, making it more representative of what we do and what we stand for. This also led to us looking at all our offerings and then designing a logo that wasn't specific to one particular offering.

## 18 Know your marketing objectives

Let's talk about marketing objectives. Obviously, you'll need to carry out a SWOT analysis, PEST analysis (more about these later), look at your target audience, your customers, your market research and your competitors, and put it all into a marketing plan with an executive summary.

After all that, the next thing you need to ask yourself about is your marketing objectives. If you do any type of marketing, what are the objectives? Are you doing it just because you've been told to do it or are you doing it for the right reasons? There could be a number of reasons why you do your marketing. The most likely one is to generate revenue.

If that's your motivation, how much revenue do you want to generate within a certain time? If your marketing plan is for three months, how much revenue do you want to generate in that time? If your objectives are to increase customer base or footfall at your event or workshop, the question is: what do you need to do to achieve that?

What works for me in marketing terms is to put on as many events as possible. I find that free events and seminars are a great way of reaching your target audience. But it depends who they are and what their backgrounds are. For a firm like ours, PR events like coffee mornings, networking events and a Christmas party all bring in business.

At these events, people bring other people, mingle and talk and we're always in front of mind. How many of those would you want to do? The key thing is to look at the marketing objectives and ask if you're able to score that way. What is the goal and how can you reach it? You have to put down realistic figures and make sure that you can actually deliver them.

But perhaps your marketing objectives are to land major clients. If so, how many and by when? Perhaps you want to become a market leader. If so, how are you going to do that? Your marketing objectives have to be SMART. That is to say Specific, Measurable, Achievable, Realistic and Time-based.

So every time you do any marketing activity – even if it's just an email activity for a few months – make sure you make it SMART as well. Oh, and BHAG – naturally. Ensure that your email campaigns and networking events always have an objective.

Your financial objectives are also very important when marketing your business, organisation or product, because your marketing will help you drive the sales. So, what is your financial objective? To increase sales? By how much? It might be by percentage or cost – but by when? Can you achieve these goals? Above all, always make your financial goals realistic.

# Three: Clients and collaboration

*"A satisfied customer is the best business strategy of all."*
**Michael LeBoeuf**

## 19 Know your customers and clients

In one of my recent workshops, I asked delegates the following question: do you know who your customers and clients are? Specifically, can you tell me who they are in a snapshot?

- ☐ Are they small businesses?
- ☐ Are they self-employed?
- ☐ Are they business start-ups?

One delegate answered, "My clients are small businesses in the East of London". But I wanted a more-specific answer.

I told him that 'small businesses in the East of London' was too wide a category. Postcodes range from E1 to E18. If he needed to advertise to these clients, would he advertise in all the papers in East London? Would he have to attend all the networking events in East London? Would he speak to all the small businesses in East London?

This is way too wide. The trick is to drill down and focus on one particular area. How you market your services to small businesses in E1 could be completely different from businesses in E10.

He answered: "Well, I'm not marketing myself very well and I'm concerned that if I go too narrow and just market what I do in just one area, I'll lose business."

I told him that wouldn't happen. I explained that I wasn't telling him not to include all the businesses in East London.

I was saying he might have to adopt a different marketing strategy for each area. I said it's better to narrow your focus, and concentrate on one area by researching, implementing and evaluating, and then move on to another area.

All of these can run parallel to what you're doing in one area. You can have several vehicles going at the same time, but you need to ensure that the vehicle you have running is the right one to serve and reach your target market. You have to find the best ways of marketing to each niche audience and then ensure you're providing the right solution to their needs.

So, you have to find the actual and not potential customer or client. You're looking for the actual customer who is going to be interested in purchasing your product or your service. Always target those who will present you with the best opportunity to get a return on your marketing.

## 20 Always have primary and secondary target audiences

When I advise business owners and entrepreneurs, I say to them: always have a primary and secondary target audience. Your primary customers and clients are the ones who will keep your shop open and busy every day – the ones who will ensure you get your bills paid every day, no matter the circumstances – and your secondary target audience.

**Here's how it works.**
To maximise the idea of the local area perspective, just imagine the world is confined to an island that's no longer than two miles. You can't leave this island, as this is the extent of the world.

Now, imagine there are just 250 people living on this island. Out of that 250, 125 are your primary target audience. You know that at least 125 of the people on this island buy your products and services on a daily basis without fail, as they need what you have to offer to survive. You can rely on them day in and day out.

Your secondary target audience are the other 125 people who don't know your business or products. However, they could become your customers or clients, too, if you knew how to reach them and market to them.

What you need to do is conduct research to find out everything you need to know about them so that you can reach them and market your offerings. In business, always have a primary and secondary target audience – it will help you to thrive and grow, as well as sustain yourself through bad weather.

## 21 Increase your marketing efforts...and have the know-how

Many of you reading this book today are probably already in business. I would say to you: look at your existing customer/client base because you can use them to conduct research or fine-tune your existing marketing plan.

Your marketing strategy and efforts must focus on particular areas that will grow your business or brand. Ask yourself if you can plan and implement a strategy. If you work from home, do you have the resources to plan, implement and evaluate your activity and efforts? If not, how are you going to do this?

If you're office based but don't have the capacity for implementation, do you need to bring in a marketing agency? Do you have the funds to take on an agency? Or are you going to employ someone?

The other day, I was speaking to someone who had been in business for over eight years. He admitted to me that marketing was not his forte, so he brought in an expert. Within six months, he had to let the person go for a number of reasons. One: he was so reliant on this person bringing in business within a few months of them starting. Two: he didn't set aside a budget for various marketing activities.

So, when the marketing expert presented a list of what the company could do to increase sales, he couldn't fund it. When the owner had brought the marketer in, he didn't set clear marketing objectives. It was like getting in a car without enough petrol to take you on your full journey. This is why you need to think about all of these areas before you even start. Remember the famous saying: if you fail to plan, you plan to fail.

## 22 Conduct a regular SWOT Analysis

Knowing your strengths and weaknesses is a vital component of succeeding in business.

In terms of your marketing experience, what are your strengths? Are you good at networking, public speaking or social media?

Conducting a SWOT analysis helps you look at or review your organisation's strengths and weaknesses, specifically in marketing.

Let me share something very personal with you. I'm the type of person who believes in sharing experiences, good or bad. I think that interacting with people who've done something and learned something from it is how we get where we want to go.

We conducted a SWOT analysis to attract and win business and improve communication with our existing clients. We had discovered that we could become more specific and direct in targeting our audiences.

We had also won a lot of business from our existing clients over the years, and they frequently recommended us to someone else. So we wanted to build a relationship with our previous and current client base and create and win new business opportunities.

This is what we found out about our business.

**Our strengths and opportunities**
We had a eight-year track record of providing specific support and specialist advice. We had a strong position in the marketplace. We were very good at delivering promotion in the field for clients – we knew how to reach out and communicate with local communities.

We had built up an excellent portfolio of clients, especially in the public sector, and had won a lot of contracts over the years. We were in the top three of the agencies who delivered the same or similar sort of services (our competitors) and, lastly, research showed that the current industry we were in (reaching diverse and hard-to-reach communities) was at conception stage and was a growing market sector.

For example, if Coca-Cola did a campaign in the US to target diverse and hard-to-reach audiences, they would aim for all communities with specific marketing activity that would engage these audiences without hesitation. They would run specific campaigns to reach Hispanics, African Americans etc.

In the UK, around only 2% of organisations do this kind of targeted marketing. Therefore, the area we specialise in is still relatively new. It's a market that's growing, too, as official statistics state that, by 2051, 20% of the UK population will be from a diverse ethnic background.

This means that when you're trying to promote your business, brand or services to non-English-speaking communities or new arrivals, there will be many barriers, such as language, in your way. Organisations are slowly starting specifically to target these areas now and not wait until 2051. Companies such as ours can help such organisations reach such audiences effectively. Well before 2051, we have the census. This will reveal the overall population of people living in the UK, including those from diverse and hard-to-reach backgrounds. I believe these figures will put our business in a good position to grow.

Apart from these many small businesses, sole traders and social enterprises are also seeing the need to market themselves beyond just placing a small advert in the local paper.

**Our weaknesses**
Now let's take a look at the weaknesses we identified. One of them involved meeting potential clients who were large corporations or major public-sector players (local councils). On several occasions, we would trek a couple of hours for a three- or four-hour meeting. Then, just when a contract was about to be agreed and signed, the person we were dealing with would leave the company. They would hand over to someone else and we'd have to start all over again.

These meetings and numerous conversations would normally amount to us winning no business. This happened on numerous occasions, so we revisited this area and now don't spend hours on end running to meetings when large corporations or councils click their fingers. We now ask for full briefs along with budgets.

Another weakness was a lack of strategy in our forward planning. We didn't take our time and really think things through when planning our business development and growth.

We also had an issue with the services we were delivering and the audiences we were serving. Our marketing literature and information didn't make it clear who we were serving, as our clients included small businesses and corporate organisations.

We delivered a different type of service to each, and both had to be marketed to differently – marketing materials had to be more tailor-made. Large corporations reading our leaflets or visiting our website might think we couldn't help them, as we help only small businesses. Likewise, small businesses thought we ran campaigns only for large corporates wanting to reach diverse audiences.

This wasn't the case, as we work with SMEs and large corporates alike – our effective marketing and PR was not aimed at a specific audience or group. It became confusing.

We were also not monitoring and evaluating our finances very well, so we couldn't see where we had or had not made profit. Our cashflow forecasts were not cashflow forecasts, credit control was poor and we never kept our books up to date. So, at the end of each financial year, the accountants tripled our bill because they had to unravel our mess before they could produce a set of accounts that made sense to Her Majesty's Revenue and Customs (HMRC).

Finance was and still is my greatest weakness, but I got around this by attending basic financial courses, hiring a book-keeper and ensuring we keep our books up to date on a regular basis, with cashflow also regularly monitored. But why am I talking about finances while discussing marketing? Well, without the finance, there's no money to conduct any kind of marketing.

Another weakness you might identify with was pricing. For a very long time, we were undercharging because we wanted to be competitive in our marketplace. This meant never refusing business even if the money was a lot lower than what we wanted. After some thorough research, we realised that undercharging was harming our business and we changed our pricing structure ASAP.

Other weaknesses included a lack of advertising in trade

publications. Our pot wasn't overflowing for advertising in trade and national magazines, and we knew from research that these platforms were the best routes to reach our corporate clients.

To add to all this came the 2009 recession, the effects of which still persist in a long, slow recovery. We lost quite a few corporate clients from the public sector, so we have now shifted our marketing efforts to target more private-sector organisations wanting to reach diverse markets.

We have also driven our efforts to reaching small businesses, sole traders and social enterprises. So much so that, in 2010, we increased profits by at least 5%, despite the downturn. The key to this success and weathering the economic storm was in doing our SWOT homework.

### Our threats
What were the threats to our business? New competition emerging and also potential clients still dealing with being in a recession. This restricts their budgets, making spending nil in some areas.

### Do your own SWOT
The SWOT analysis really helped my company to focus and omit what was not working for us. But instead of drowning my sorrows on my company's weaknesses, I worked tirelessly to turn our weaknesses around, which is why I'm here today, writing a book that shares my experiences and learnings.

So that was my company's SWOT analysis. What's yours?

Take this opportunity to do your own, using a SWOT analysis template. Here's mine, which you're welcome to use.

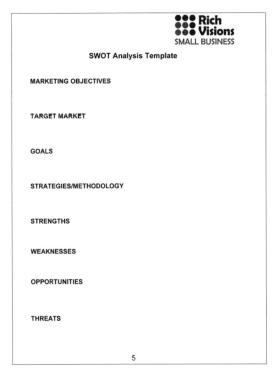

You can complete the top sections if you want but, for now, just think about your strengths and weaknesses in terms of your marketing and promotion. What do you think your strengths are? What do you know already? What don't you know? What areas do you think you need to improve on? What opportunities do you think are out there and what threats are there?

## 23 Conduct a situation analysis

Whether you're currently in full-time employment and looking to start a business or you've been in business for two or three years, you need to look at the current situation – the state of the union, the market that you're in.

Has there been growth or decline? Now look at your business.

Perhaps you've been going for three years or so and things seem to be going well. Perhaps you've just started up? What are your offerings? Have you got any new offerings? Assess your competitors and advantages against your offerings as well.

This is your Situation Analysis – a look at the current climate just before you start your marketing. Now think about what you know about the market already. What opportunities are out there? Summarise the market research.

What are you selling? It might be an event or a service. Whatever it is, you need to look at the price. Whatever they're selling, lots of organisations are charging the wrong price. Don't be one of them – be clear about where you fit into the marketplace.

## 24 Understand the importance of conducting a PEST analysis

The PEST analysis should be part of your strategic planning and/or market research. It stands for:

Political – how and to what degree the government will intervene in or affect the economy.

Economic – factors including the rate of inflation, economic growth, exchange rates and interest rates.

Social – population growth rate, cultural patterns, attitudes to work and changing social trends.

Technological – factors including technological changes, research and development activity and automation.

A PEST analysis takes into account the external factors that could affect your business. It's a useful strategic tool for understanding the growth (or decline) in your market, your business position, and the potential and direction for your business.

For example, a recession may have a detrimental effect on your business if you sell luxury goods. That's because, when a recession hits, people normally pay for their needs and not their wants or desires.

# Four: PR and publicity

*"Publicity can be terrible – but only if you don't have any."*
**Jane Russell**

## 25 Understand the power of PR

Before we go any further, let's agree what's meant by PR. Public Relations is about using the media to raise your profile, build your reputation, and promote your brand or image. PR has helped many small businesses to grow, and it can help yours, too. It helps you retain current clients or customers, increase sales, win new business, boost profits, and keep ahead of your competitors.

PR looks at your long-term and short-term goals for developing your business's brand, and also looks at reaching your target audience direct, from a wider perspective.

PR also helps boost your brand by creating news and stories that get you press coverage. PR is a marketing tool – a cost-effective and powerful one. However, PR is not an alternative to advertising. Instead, it goes hand-in-hand with advertising.

**What are the advantages of PR?**
PR is ideal for new and existing businesses. It's ideal if you have only a small budget, and it gives you an opportunity to reach a wider audience. The disadvantages of PR are that chasing up press and press releases, and following up with reporters, is all very time-consuming.

PR isn't a one-off activity – it has to be ongoing, and it's also not strictly free because it does involve a lot of time. The other thing about PR is that your press coverage might not always be free.

In simple terms, PR is a media game. It's about composing a press release, article or feature, and sending it to the right publication. The media is virtually unlimited in terms of publications that are out there across the different segments of the media.

Media could range from trade, business, diaspora, women, trade, regional, and national press. This gives you the opportunity to let your actual and potential customers and clients see and hear what you have to offer and reach over a million people in one PR campaign.

Over the last few years, I've had over 80 features across the different press. They've helped me to secure over £2 million worth of business. It's been interesting and challenging, but the end result has been a success story: we've won a lot of business and contracts through continuous PR, getting as much coverage as possible.

## 26 Identify your target audiences for PR

Many organisations are unable to identify the type of media titles and publications that their target audience reads.

You must be able to identify who your customers and clients are before looking at PR opportunities. You need to know all the ins and outs of your customers. Where do they live? How old are they? What are their occupations? What other products do they consume? What publications do they read? Where can you find them? Try to understand everything about your customer or your client.

As I've indicated, I always advise people to divide their market into primary and secondary audiences. Who are you primary audiences, your bread and butter audiences that you need to reach out to on a regular basis to keep your brand or your product in front of your customers' minds and pay the bills? Identify who your ideal customer is.

And your secondary audience? These are the people you *could* target who could be new customers or clients from a new market that you are not targeting.

So the challenge is to identify who your customers are and where they live. If you're selling a product, then obviously you want to look at what their spending power is and whether they'd be interested in your product.

Over the years, people in business have said to me that they don't actually know who their customers are. Or maybe they'll tell me that their customers are people in the whole of London. Not a problem at all, except that if you've just started a business, targeting the whole of London is probably outside the scope of your marketing budget.

I'm not saying that you can't target them, but you do need to have a specific target audience that you know well, that you understand, and that you can market to with your eyes closed. So you could market to many people.

Many of you reading this book may be women, but you're all probably from different backgrounds and have different lifestyles. It's all about building your target audience over time and continuing to do so, each day.

And remember: think big and think BHAG.

### Who are your ideal clients?

In 2008, my company's primary customers were public-sector organisations in the UK – central government, to be precise. They wanted to target diverse audiences and, from previous research we had conducted, we knew people in this sector working in marketing and communications read papers like

*The Guardian, Marketing* and *PR Week*. We focused our efforts on gaining publicity in these papers and I'm proud to say that we made it into these papers. Here's the proof:

*Left: The Guardian,*

*Top: The Trumpet, Above: PR Week*

For our other company, Rich Visions Small Business, we also knew that most of our clients were from ethnic minority backgrounds, so any PR was aimed at ethnic media titles such as *The Voice, Eastern Eye, etc*. We also looked at business publications and, again, I am proud to say that we gained publicity in these media, too, over time.

## 27 Always have a PR and publicity plan

A PR plan is a vital part of your armoury. What does the PR plan do? It summarises where you are now, looking at all the PR and publicity that you've conducted since you started the business or from when you started doing marketing and PR. It also looks at where you'd like to be.

One of my biggest challenges about five years into my business was that I wanted to get into the trade press. I finally got into PR Week and then I wanted to get into the nationals and, finally, I made *The Guardian* in 2010. It wasn't easy but I had a plan and I achieved that plan.

The PR plan also looks at your target customers and clients, creating an action plan and timeline, and setting budgets. This is where you determine how much it's going to cost you to do your own PR over a period of time, or whether it's worth hiring an agency to do your PR.

Once you think about all your needs, wants and desires for your PR and publicity plan, you then look at what tools you are going to use to get the publicity you want and measure the success of your PR, which is very important.

Imagine for a moment you need to travel 250 miles to another city with your three-month-old baby. You'd want to make the journey as smooth and comfortable as possible for your baby. You'd need to think about all the things you need to get to that city, such as having petrol in your car, checking the car's in good shape, and packing all the necessary items for the baby and yourself. You can use a scenario like this as a stir to think about and plan your PR and publicity.

## 28 Determine the elements of your PR plan

What are the objectives of your plan and the results you expect to see? For example, the objective for our PR plan in 2009 was to raise the profile of the company, Rich Visions, to become one of the UK's leading agencies and consultancies for those wishing to target and reach diverse communities.

Even though we were a leading agency, we really wanted to stand out from our competitors and keep the brand front of mind to our target audiences.

One of the key points of our strategy is that we are the only agency to provide solutions under one roof. This means that, apart from helping people to reach diverse audiences, we also offer training and consultancy, which our competitors don't.

We wanted to intensify our competitiveness, building different messages, unique selling points and angles for ourselves so that we can gain as much coverage as possible. We wanted to target media that we knew our target audience engages with across national, trade, specialist, regional and diaspora media.

## 29 Use the vertical media

You should also look at the vertical press. What's that? Vertical press means media from the same sector, such as technology press or lifestyle press. This is a useful strategy if you work within a certain industry and have provided a lot of services, campaigns or projects.

For example, we did a PR and marketing campaign for the Sector Skills Council (Construction) and produced a case study after we completed the campaign. We showed the work we did for this organisation and the results we achieved. We then devised a list of all construction media and sent off the case study, which we tweaked into a press release, to the relevant press.

Having the story published raised the profile of our company, as well as the work we'd done in this industry. If anyone in construction was looking for this type of service, there'd now be a better chance that they'd contact us to find out more or book our services.

Please note that your PR plan is completely different from your marketing plan, even though there may be some common areas.

The great thing about having a PR plan is that you can look at the plan you had drafted six or 12 months later, and see what worked and what didn't. You can then plan for the following six to 12 months, taking into account what has worked and what you need to do to improve.

You can also look at the plan, assess the goals and objectives you set, and work out where you are now. Perhaps you said you wanted to get into three different publications: how many did you get into? Why did you not get into a particular title? Are you going to put the answers forward for your next set of PR planning, so that each time you review and evaluate your plan, you get closer to reaching your target audiences, customers or clients?

## 30 Choose the right angles to get into the press

To get into the press, you need to have a good angle or have a good story. What will be your angle to get into *The Guardian* or whatever publication or TV station you want to get into? If I were to phone up my local newspaper and say I am from Rich Visions and I want you to put me in your paper because I am based in your local area, the journalist will tell me that that isn't newsworthy.

Recently, however, we won a PR contract with one of the UK's biggest charities. We were given the opportunity to announce officially that we had won this contract in trade and specialist publications, and the news appeared in over 10 different media titles, including my business's local newspaper.

For us to get featured in this local paper, we had to think of an angle that would get us good coverage. The angle we used was quite simply that we were a local business that had just won a big contract with one of the UK's largest charities. We then had to chase up the newspaper on several occasions (editors and journalists are very busy people – get used to doing a lot of chasing, unless you have headline news for them.)

After finally getting hold of someone, we were asked if winning this contract would create jobs in the local area. We said yes and a week later we were featured in the publication. A great result.

### 31 Always prepare a media plan

If you want to get into the press, always devise a media plan. This can be drawn up on a simple spreadsheet. Just make a list of the titles you would like to see your story or news appear in. List also contact names, deadline dates and readership (for newspapers), page viewers (for the internet) viewership (for TV) and listenership (for radio) figures. You should be able to obtain these from the media titles direct.

Having a media plan can help you review what titles you did or didn't get into, as well as evaluate how successful your plan was.

Events and awareness days or weeks are good to try and get features in the media. For example, if you're a charity working with women affected by breast cancer, you can see if you can get into the right publications during Breast Cancer Month. It's that simple.

## 32 Know what makes a good story

Now that you've started your PR plan, the next thing to think about is what makes a good story. Think about different angles. Obviously, the key factors for getting coverage are current news and information that's relevant to that particular publication. Is your news relevant to that publication?

One thing you should remember is that the media have pages to fill and are always looking for content and credibility.

## 33 Use these good PR angles

Here are some angles you could use:

☐ Reaching a milestone in business: one, five, ten, 25 or 50 years in business, for example.

☐ Winning an award. We have won three awards and got press coverage for all of them just by writing a simple press release.

☐ Tips and advice on your specialist area – this is something that I think everybody should get involved in. Whatever your specialism or your expertise, try and work towards giving tips and advice on your specialist area. I currently advise on marketing and PR as well as offering business tips and advice for a few publications in the form of articles, as this raises my own and my company's profile.

☐ Publicity stunts – you might want to do a bungee jump for charity.

☐ You may have a celebrity or high-profile person from your industry attend one of your events as a guest or speaker.

☐ Charity donations? Maybe you donated money or equipment to your local children's hospice?

☐ An event you are holding that will be of interest to your target audience and the press.

☐ A new product line or range involving competitions, giveaways, promotions or BOGOFs.

☐ Interesting people in your industry or sector. If you've got someone interesting in your industry or your sector and you think the media may be interested in publishing it, that's also a good angle.

## 34 Understand the power of articles

Articles are powerful, and I've written quite a few. They include advice on using Twitter, the power of PR, e-networking, and the importance of having a business plan for small businesses.

I've also written really niche articles for my industry on how to reach diverse and hard-to-reach communities, or effective ways of reaching Muslim women, and the cost of getting your communications wrong, from an ethnic perspective.

What I love about articles is that, at the end of the article, your name and company appear with a direct contact number. This invariably will win you more business.

On the subject of awards, winning them usually prompts the

press to call with a view to an interview or special feature – another surefire way of getting great publicity and winning more business.

In the last class that I took, I went around the room and gave everyone an idea for writing to the press. Here are some examples:

- ☐ A trainer and business coach could give advice on business or tips for trainers.
- ☐ A restaurant could give tips and advice on healthy eating, healthy foods or cooking recipes.
- ☐ A fashion retailer could talk about the latest high street or contemporary fashions.
- ☐ A film-production company could talk about how to produce good-quality films.

## 35 Use publicity stunts to good effect

Here are some examples of publicity stunts you could take inspiration from.

A mainstream agency that we work with was raising money for a men's charity. All the men agreed not to shave for two weeks. Each week, they updated clients and potential clients on progress through Facebook and Twitter. Later on, they sent a press release to the trade press with photos announcing how much they raised for the charity.

Another chap I met a few years ago did a publicity stunt for his new book. He went to Trafalgar Square one afternoon with a few celebrity lookalikes, including Prince Charles and Camilla. He attracted many spectators, who enjoyed taking pictures of the lookalikes, who were holding a big sign sporting the title of his new book and date of release.

Later that day, he wrote a press release and sent it off with pictures to the national, consumer, business and local press. It didn't make the nationals, but he did receive local, regional and business-press coverage. I attended this event and can vouch for its impact – the lookalikes were very convincing.

So, the key thing is to look at what you think would work for your target audience and research what media they read as well.

## 36 Ensure your angles and media list are well targeted

When looking for media publicity, it's vital to ensure that the angles and your media list are targeted to your customers and clients. There's not much point writing a press release that will be featured in a Men and Motors magazine when your target audience is women over 75.

You have to know exactly who your chosen media are talking to, so that your marketing and PR can be focused, targeted and on-point.

Always remember, too, that your angles or stories should be really different and unique. After all, what makes a good game of darts is when you hit the bullseye.

You can also build your profile and reputation with PR beyond the media. This can include:

☐ Writing a book or e-books.

☐ Speaking at an event that you know your target audience will attend. Speaking at events allows you to showcase your business, raise awareness or win new contracts for your business *and* get noticed in the media.

☐ Public speaking and after-dinner speaking events.

☐ Hosting your own seminars and workshop (in your specialist area of expertise).

☐ Attending networking events.

[] Getting nominated for industry awards or accreditations.
[] Composing newsletters for your clients and customers for repeat business or referrals.

**Great PR success stories**

I love watching Dragon's Den because I love the Dragons' PR tactics. They're always in the limelight (good and negative spins), speak at many events and have their own books and products.

So who do I think has been the most successful Dragon in terms of PR? All of them. They're always in the public eye for the right (and sometimes wrong) reasons. Excitingly, in today's new world of communication, we have social media platforms such as Twitter and Facebook, where we can get close to people who inspire us.

Even though using personal PR is more talking about you than your brand or company, it helps to increase sales and revenue. After all, you know the famous saying – 'people buy from people'.

## 37 Get inspired by my PR success

If you're looking for some inspiration for your PR, you might want to hear about some of my own triumphs.

**Business PR**

In 2009, we nominated one of my staff (Jessica) to PR Week for 29 under 29 (that is, 29 of the most talented and promising young professionals under 29 in the PR industry). Out of over 300 applicants, Jessica was featured. It was a great opportunity to highlight the fine talent we had at our agency, Rich Visions.

**Personal PR**

I've had a number of successes with personal PR. To date, I've had no fewer than 90 pieces of coverage and over 15 TV and radio interviews – and counting.

A few years ago, I created my own personal website, www.mavisamankwah.com. The site provides information about me and my career and businesses, as well as information on my speaking engagements, workshops and seminars (I've created a bit of a following over the years).

I'm also a big fan of social media. I can use it to build a media platform and engage with my target audiences direct. I have also produced my own personal business cards, had a logo designed, created flyers, and have my own pop-up stand. These help raise my profile and brand wherever I can get the chance to promote myself, my business and my brand, as well as push my entrepreneurial skills, and inspire and encourage people like you.

People from all walks of life often approach me at events wanting to talk about their business, how they can set up their business, their marketing and their PR, and how can they make it a success. It makes me feel good to know that I'm making an impact in someone's life from a business perspective.

I also do a lot of speaking-engagement bookings where I talk about personal PR, and I also offer marketing and PR training. Personal PR has brought me small-business contracts and corporate contracts and has made me who I am today.

**My speaking opportunities**

Over the years, I've spoken at local schools, glitzy business events, church halls and other establishments. I recently spoke to young teenagers who had been excluded from school. I told them that they could set up their own business whatever their circumstances and focus on their passions, dreams and aspirations.

*Here is an example of an event I have spoken at*

# Five: Me, myself and I

*"All publicity is good, except an obituary notice."*
**Brendan Behan**

*"A PR plan is a vital part of your business armoury."*
**Mavis Amankwah**

I said this book wasn't about me. However, I believe strongly in the power of PR. Hey, you don't say – I started a PR agency! So it might help you to hear about how I managed to get myself into the media.

## How I got in to the press

### How did I make the nationals?

I've always been keen to get into the national press, especially *The Guardian*. Over the years, I'd always looked at different angles to get a presence in the nationals – and then one day it happened.

One of my staff read an interview with a chap in *The Guardian* about equality and diversity. She then vowed to get me featured in the paper and emailed the journalist from *The Guardian* who had written the article, introducing her to Rich Visions and Mavis Amankwah. After a week, we'd had no reply and were getting edgy. But we stayed patient and, sure enough, a few days later, we got a response.

The journalist said she was very keen to interview me and wanted us to send further information. Within two weeks, I was sitting in the reception of *The Guardian*'s London offices waiting to be interviewed about equality in senior management.

A week later, there I was in *The Guardian*, in a column feature on a very prominent page. This gave me great exposure and the chance to share my story with anyone trying to be featured in a national newspaper.

The moral of the story is that it's not hard to get into the media. Just be consistent and always follow stories, contact journalists and editors, and don't forget to chase them up.

Since then, the journalist has made a point of keeping in touch and I always send her press releases. Who knows – one day we might get another opportunity.

**How did I get into PR Week?**

Another personal PR success was making the pages of PR Week. After attending a few of their awards ceremonies, conferences and events, I'd managed to build up a bit of a relationship with some of the journalists there.

In 2007, I invited one of the journalists to attend our business's fifth-anniversary event in London. The journalist came down and had a really great time (as well as finding out about our company and our future plans). Eight months after the event (it pays to be patient in this game), the journalist wrote a double-page-spread feature on Rich Visions. The article talked about communications, the ethnic population, diversity, and, of course, me.

To take out a similar-sized double-page advertisement would have cost around £5,000. That's the value of great PR.

The PR Week feature was a really big one that won me loads of business. This included a contract from a large UK charity and a local authority. To this day, people still tell me they saw my feature in PR Week and that my interview was interesting.

The other good thing about features is that you can refer to them in your brochures and other marketing materials.

These days, we always send PR Week press releases on any new contracts or business accounts we have – and, nine times out of ten, they'll publish them. The key tactic with the media is to build up relationships with the journalists and editors.

### How did I get into business magazines?
I've been featured in quite a few business magazines. I mostly talk about the contracts my company has won, and about entrepreneurship and marketing and PR advice for small businesses.

One particular magazine focused solely on contracts. They asked me questions about how I win contracts and, in particular, public-sector contracts. They did a whole case study about a contract that I won a few years ago – how I applied, how I wrote tenders, the ITTs (Invitations to Tender), the PQQs (Pre-Qualification Questionnaire) and so on. I talked them through all that and the result was a big feature on contracts, my business and myself.

After that interview, I was approached by another three or four business publications. These interviews and features often generate lots of spin-offs.

### How did I get into ethnic publications?
I normally get into these type of publications because of my ethnicity. Many of the publications that I've succeeded with, such as The Voice, The Trumpet and African Voices, have been ethnicity-focused.

### How did I get into regional publications?
Regional press coverage is usually easier to get than national press. Regional press like to hear about what local businesses are doing about business growth and helping the local community. I've been featured in *The Newham Recorder* on numerous occasions.

The area is an excellent location to be in because our offices are close to the main site of the 2012 Olympics. The area also has a huge shopping centre (Westfields), a local airport, and one of the UK's biggest sugar factories (Tate & Lyle). A few miles down the road sits Canary Wharf, too – so our local paper has lots of news to report.

The paper wrote a piece about me winning an award and has given me editorials on some of the free local business seminars we have run.

**Other features**
I've been featured on being a mum, juggling a business and personal life. Christian channels have featured me because of my faith. One TV station interviewed me with a view to encouraging Christian women to set up their own businesses.

I've given advice on the advantages and disadvantages of PR for small businesses, too. This was a live show, with people calling in and asking questions about everything from juggling family life and business to how to start a business. You can still see this interview on YouTube today – just search for my name.

## 38 Learn how to write an effective press release

When sending a press release, make sure you get the journalist or editor's name right, as well as the correct contact number, before sending out the releases. Don't address your press release to 'The Editor' – personalise it where you can.

You should avoid using jargon and technical words to describe what you do. Send out news and events and stories on a regular basis as you never know when the press might be interested in your press release, news or story. Remember: the media are always hungry for good content.

Always ensure you meet the press deadline and limit your press release to about 300 words, with no more than 60 sentences. Ensure also that you put any notes about your company, service or product in the Notes to the Editor section at the end and not in the body of the email.

Notes to the Editor can include information about your company, who you are, what you do, your telephone number, and similar information.

## Writing a press release

When writing a press release, always include a date. If you want the release to be embargoed (this means that the press can't publish it before a certain date), write Embargo and the appropriate date at the top.

Make it clear what your communication is by writing Press Release clearly at the top, with an attention-grabbing headline or factual information. This will help the editor or journalist to identify what the release is about within a few seconds.

You should place the key information in the first few paragraphs of the release, trying to incorporate the who, what, where, why and when into the first paragraph. Put whatever it is you're trying to say or promote in the first few paragraphs.

Always try to add a quote if you are writing about a person and, if someone is coming to an event as a guest speaker, get a quote from them, such as:

Always tweak press releases accordingly to the specific publication or medium.

## Imagery

When trying to secure a feature with imagery, always ensure you send high-resolution pictures with clear written captions (*see page 58*). If you are sending imagery of people taken by a professional photographer, always give credit to the photographer where possible. Add any quotes.

### 39 Avoid your press releases going in the bin

Too many press releases end up in the editor's bin. There are a number of reasons for that. Let's look at a few of them:

- The release was too long, with no interesting information.
- The pictures were not clear.
- There were no quotes.
- The story was buried in the last paragraph, and the editor didn't have time to read through it.
- The deadline was missed.
- The press release wasn't personalised.
- The editor's name was spelt wrongly and it had lots of grammar and spelling mistakes.

**Contacting the press**
Occasionally, it's a good idea to give the publications a call and ask them what features they have coming up, as it might be possible to get your name or the business's name mentioned in them.

# Six: Evolution and evaluation

*"To refuse awards is another way of accepting them with more noise than is normal."*

**Peter Ustinov**

## 40 Make an effort to win awards

Winning awards raises your profile. It helps your business evolve. To date, I have won three awards and have been a finalist in three others. We've been nominated or referred for awards by business associates, which has helped us to build our reputation and raise our profile across our industry.

## 41 Build on social media

We've also built recognition on the social-media platform for all our brands. Social media, such as Twitter, Facebook and LinkedIn, is the growing phenomenon in business and, if you're not on it, you could be missing out on a huge number of new clients or customers.

For some of you, your target audience may not be people who are based on the Internet. However, I think for most of us today, our target audiences do access the Web and some form of social media as well.

These days, even grannies and grandads are on Facebook – they're using social media to see pictures of their grandchildren on the other side of the world, and dialling in to Skype to speak to them.

## YouTube

At Rich Visions, we've got a YouTube account. I think all businesses should have one. You can showcase a 30-second advert or even feature your events, workshops or seminars. Just put up a few two- to three-minute clips to capture your audiences. Remember: each PR activity you do must have an objective, so if you're going to use YouTube, ask yourself why.

At most of the events we host, we normally take clips and put them on YouTube. You can see how many times they've been viewed and by whom.

## Twitter

Twitter is the new social-media sensation. It's a great way of keeping your clients abreast of new developments in the business and also of winning new customers. I tweet about my business, and sometimes my personal life, and my number of followers continues to grow daily. I offer information on business sustainability, marketing and PR, as well as thoughts for the day and opinions on the latest happenings in my industry and beyond.

## LinkedIn

I love LinkedIn. It's a great tool for reuniting with clients, customers and business associates and keeping each other informed of work, projects, events and campaigns especially from a business-to-business perspective

You can debate business topics with others, add an attractive profile, link to your website and so on. LinkedIn is a good tool, especially for business communications, and it's free.

## Blog

One thing a business blog isn't is a diary of daily activities.

That's the territory of a personal blog. Instead, think of your business blog as another arm of your online marketing. You can use it in a number of ways, but the key element is mutual communication with clients and potential clients, as well as business development.

One happy side-effect of your business blog is that Google will thank you for it. The search engines love to see a site that's alive and being populated with new, relevant content. For anyone for whom search-engine optimisation is a factor, a blog is a must. So start one today and pepper it with relevant keywords.

## 42 Plan your activity

Planning should be the main thing you do before implementing any type of activity, whether it's social media or speaking at an after-dinner event. For each activity you plan to do, you need to ask yourself a few questions.

What's the idea or plan? What's the objective of the activity – for example, are you joining LinkedIn because you want to get more contacts? When do you want to start and end this activity, or is it ongoing? How much is it going to cost? Is there a deadline?

If you want to get into the media, you need to know the precise media timings and deadlines. There's no point in phoning someone at a local paper if they're on a deadline, as they won't have time to talk to you. You also need to be aware of deadlines for any press release or news feature you have planned.

Once you've started planning your activity, you must think about implementation (who will do a particular activity or task?), as well as evaluations (looking at what has worked and what hasn't). You need to evaluate the planned activity beforehand and set aside a budget.

## 43 Evaluate campaigns online

What I like about online is that you can clearly measure results quite quickly. For example, you can see the numbers of people accessing your site with a simple software tool such as Google Analytics, which is easy to set up and use.

Or, let's say you did an email marketing campaign. With a simple piece of software, you can see who is opening, deleting, or unsubscribing to your emails, as well as looking at who revisits your website and which pages they look at.

I know a company that will email or call you and say that they've seen you looking at a particular page on their website several times. They ask you if they can help you, as they can see you could be a potential customer.

## 44 Evaluate your marketing and PR plans

Sometimes, measuring the success or efficiency of your marketing or PR plans can be difficult. That's especially true if you're using a number of tactics all at the same time or if you do business through networking and contacts. I know I keep going on about it, but this is why your plans should always be SMART (Specific, Measurable, Achievable, Realistic and Timebound).

If you stick to the SMART model, you'll have plans that can easily be monitored and measured.

**Ask yourself**

**As a starting point:**

- ☐ Have your sales or income increased or decreased over a certain period of time?
- ☐ Do you know how your existing clients found you?
- ☐ Did the marketing or PR plan you implemented last quarter give you direct responses? If so, how many?
- ☐ Have the endless networking events you've been attending created business opportunities (sales, contacts, referrals)?
- ☐ Did the money you invested to implement your PR plan provide a good ROI (return on investment)?

There are other ways that you can measure your marketing and PR campaigns. Here are a few examples:

- ☐ The number of telephone responses you received from your last email shot.
- ☐ Feedback from the product giveaway competition you ran in your local newspaper or magazine.
- ☐ Write special coding on your publicity materials so, when people call or email you to respond, they quote this code, so you know where that publicity material was distributed.
- ☐ The total number of newspapers and magazines that you or your brand were featured in for free (PR).
- ☐ The number of hits to your website from a dedicated page displaying an offer or service (special promotion).

☐ The number of questionnaires and surveys you received from existing customers or clients.
☐ Year-on-year sales growth.
☐ The number of contacts you collected at the pet show (for example) you exhibited at.

You need to be able to evaluate what has worked and what hasn't. Every marketing and PR activity must have an objective ('Why I am going to do an email shot this month and how will I measure it?').

Remember: 50% of marketing and advertising is wasted, but it's being able to work out *which* 50% that's the key. The more you tailor and measure your success, the more you'll be able to invest in what really works. So, ditch what doesn't work and increase those profits.

# Seven: In summary

*"I've failed over and over and over again in my life and that is why I succeed."*

## Michael Jordan

I hope you've found this short guide to using PR and marketing to grow your business useful. Hopefully, you can learn and draw strength from my own experiences in increasing my profile and expanding my marketing and publicity efforts.

It's a tough world out there for a fledgling business, and it's only getting tougher. Only the right mindset will see you through. See every day as a new opportunity. Try to imagine that this is the day when you win your biggest contract ever – and try to make it happen. This isn't the Post Office, where you wait for delivery. Be proactive: the world won't come to you.

On a practical level, think strategically and plan, plan, plan. Plan your PR campaigns; plan your marketing campaigns. Execute them professionally – using professionals. Then evaluate, evaluate, evaluate. What went well? What could you have done better?

Understand your finances, without becoming your own book-keeper. Diversify if the market changes, without entering totally unfamiliar territory. Make contacts. Network. Make smart use of social media. Make a big effort to get into the press. Say to yourself: this is the year when I make the printed media three times. It can be done, it's virtually free, and it's like dynamite for your business.

Finally, never neglect your personal life. Business success is important. However, success in business is like a pebble next to the Ayers Rock that is your friends and family. Never imagine that when your business gets big that that's the time to get your social life back again. Having your social life in balance is crucial in business, especially if you have children or are married, or your family is reliant on you.

Similarly, don't neglect your health and wellbeing. Keep up that gym membership – your mind works better in a healthy body. Time spent on a treadmill is also great creative thinking time. If you're fit, you'll also have less time off sick – which can only mean more profits.

So, keep your chin up, keep pushing hard during the tough times, keep yourself active and, above all, keep thinking BHAG.

Good luck.

**Mavis Amankwah**

## About Mavis

Mavis Amankwah is an entrepreneur specialising in marketing, PR and diversity communications. Winner of three business awards and a full member of the Chartered Institute of PR (CIPR), she's regularly named by PR Week as one of the 'most influential people in PR' and has been featured in over 70 press titles.

Mavis's business story began in 2002, when she spotted a gap in the market and Rich Visions (www.richvisions.co.uk) was born, helping organisations communicate with diverse and hard-to-reach communities.

In 2009, realising that small businesses were not consistently using marketing and PR, Mavis launched another arm of the agency (www.richvisionssb.co.uk), which has helped over 200 businesses to grow.

Year on year, Rich Visions has itself grown. In this indispensable handbook, Mavis draws on her own experience at the sharp end of business to offer would-be and actual entrepreneurs, to whom this book is dedicated, advice on growing their businesses.